This is Daniel Cook
at the Construction Site

Kids Can Press

This is Daniel Cook.
He likes to go different places,
meet interesting people
and try new things.

Mostly I like to have fun!

Today Daniel is visiting a construction site.

Here we are!

This is Chris. Chris is a construction worker. He's going to show Daniel how to build a sidewalk.

At a construction site, everyone wears safety equipment. Hard hats are made of very strong plastic. They protect construction workers' heads from hits and bumps.

Workers also wear brightly colored safety vests to make sure they can see one another. Gloves and steel-toed boots protect workers' hands and feet.

Construction workers keep you safe, too! They put fences and signs around the construction site to warn of danger. And they make a path where people can walk safely until the new sidewalk is ready.

Before the construction workers can build the new sidewalk, they have to clear away the old one. They use a machine called a backhoe.

A backhoe is a digger. It breaks the sidewalk into concrete slabs and loads them into a dump truck. It can lift HUGE pieces of concrete that weigh *thousands* of pounds!

Maybe I could borrow the backhoe to clean my room...

Domenic is a backhoe operator. He's giving Daniel some tips. The main controls for a backhoe are a pair of joysticks. One joystick moves the boom and swings the hoe. The other joystick moves the stick and opens and closes the bucket.

These look like computer game controllers.

The hoe is built like your arm. Its boom works like your upper arm, its stick works like your forearm and its bucket works like your hand.

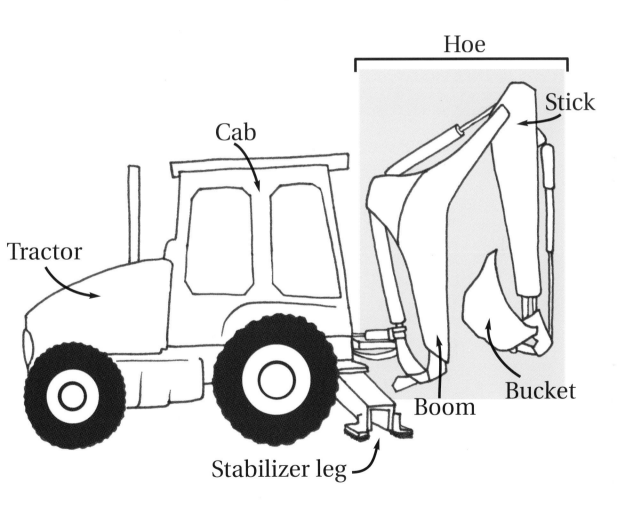

Hoe

Cab

Stick

Tractor

Boom

Bucket

Stabilizer leg

First we lower the bucket to the sidewalk by moving the boom and the stick.

Next we open the bucket to dig into the concrete. Once we get a chunk, we close the bucket to hold it tight.

Then we swing the hoe and raise the bucket over the dump truck. Opening the bucket unloads the concrete.

Let's do it again!

Now that the backhoe has cleared the big chunks of concrete, Daniel helps the construction workers rake up the small pieces left behind and shovel them into wheelbarrows.

It's hard work!

Next come the wooden forms. The workers cut and join pieces of wood that will frame the wet concrete.

Just like a cake pan holds batter, the wooden forms will hold and shape the wet concrete. Sidewalks are usually made up of many square or rectangular slabs of concrete.

Cool! I'd love to have a birthday cake that big!

Now we're ready for the concrete!

Concrete is made up of water, sand, tiny stones and cement. The cement works like glue. It binds, or sticks, all these ingredients together.

Concrete has been around for thousands of years. It is the perfect building material because its ingredients are easy to find, it's easy to shape and it lasts a long time.

All kinds of structures are built with concrete, such as highways, overpasses, buildings and poles. The world's largest concrete structure is under construction in China. The Three Gorges Dam on the Yangtze River will stretch over 2.3 km (1.4 mi.) long.

That's almost two thousand Daniels lined up head to toe!

Here comes the concrete mixer!

If you've ever seen a concrete mixer driving along, you probably noticed that its drum is always spinning. Do you know why? Concrete sets quickly. If the drum doesn't turn, the wet concrete inside will harden before the truck arrives at the construction site.

THAT would be
one big mess!

A turning drum
keeps the concrete
wet and soft so it's
easy to pour.

As the concrete is poured, the workers use different tools to even it out quickly. They use rakes to drag the concrete into place. Then they smooth the surface with floats and edgers.

Oops — missed a spot!

When the sidewalk finally looks smooth, the workers use brooms to rough up the surface again! Why? The broom marks on sidewalks grip the bottoms of your shoes as you walk so you won't slip if the sidewalk is wet.

Slipping is for slides — not sidewalks!

The last step in sidewalk building is to set, or cure, the concrete. To set a cake, you bake it in the oven. To set concrete, you can coat it with a special liquid seal or cover it with sheets of plastic or wet burlap. Curing protects the sidewalk surface and makes it stronger.

The next day the
new sidewalk is open!

Look out sidewalk.
Here I come!

Footprints in wet concrete wreck a sidewalk's finish, so here's a way to leave your mark without getting into trouble! Just remember: You have to work fast, or the plaster will harden. Ask a grown-up to help you.

You will need
- 250 – 500 mL plaster of Paris 1 – 2 cups
- 250 mL water 1 cup
- an old container (a margarine or yogurt tub works well)
- a popsicle stick or an old spatula
- an aluminum pie plate
- decorations, such as beads, wooden letters, small toys, glitter

1. Cover your work surface with newspaper.

2. Pour the water into the container.

3. Stir in the plaster of Paris until the mixture is as thick and creamy as a milkshake.

4. Quickly pour the plaster into the pie plate. Gently shake the plate till the surface is even.

5. Carefully press your hand into the plaster. Keep still for about 30 seconds. Remove your hand.

6. If you like, press decorations into the plaster.

7. Let the plaster dry overnight. (If you'd like to paint it, wait 4 days.)

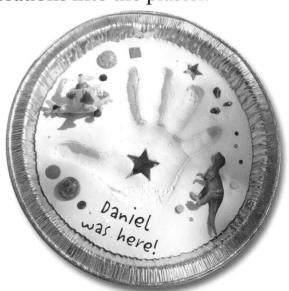

Based on the TV series *This is Daniel Cook*. Concept created by J.J. Johnson and Blair Powers. Produced by marblemedia and Sinking Ship Productions Inc.

Kids Can Press acknowledges the financial support of the Government of Ontario, through the Ontario Media Development Corporation's Ontario Book Initiative; the Ontario Arts Council; the Canada Council for the Arts; and the Government of Canada, through the BPIDP, for our publishing activity.

The producers of *This is Daniel Cook* acknowledge the support of Treehouse TV, TVOntario, other broadcast and funding partners and the talented, hard-working crew that made *This is Daniel Cook* a reality. In addition, they acknowledge the support and efforts of Deb, Murray and the Cook family, as well as Karen Boersma, Sheila Barry and Valerie Hussey at Kids Can Press.

Published in Canada by
Kids Can Press Ltd.
29 Birch Avenue
Toronto, ON M4V 1E2

Published in the U.S. by
Kids Can Press Ltd.
2250 Military Road
Tonawanda, NY 14150

www.kidscanpress.com

Written by Yvette Ghione
Edited by Karen Li
Illustrations and design by Céleste Gagnon
With special thanks to Domenic Fuoco and Construction Supervisor Chris Myers of the City of Toronto.

Printed and bound in Singapore

The hardcover edition of this book is smyth sewn casebound.
The paperback edition of this book is limp sewn with a drawn-on cover.

Kids Can Press is a *Corus*™ Entertainment company

CM 07 0 9 8 7 6 5 4 3 2 1
CM PA 07 0 9 8 7 6 5 4 3 2 1

Visit Daniel online at **www.thisisdanielcook.com**

Library and Archives Canada Cataloguing in Publication

Ghione, Yvette
     This is Daniel Cook at the Construction Site / written by Yvette Ghione.

ISBN-13: 978-1-55453-083-0 (bound)
ISBN-10: 1-55453-083-0 (bound)
ISBN-13: 978-1-55453-084-7 (pbk.)
ISBN-10: 1-55453-084-9 (pbk.)

1. Building sites—Juvenile literature. 2. Sidewalks—Design and construction—Juvenile literature. I. Title.

TE280.G49 2007   j624   C2006-902264-X

Photo Credits